INDIGO ANIMAL™

Rue Harris

PORCH LION PRESS
PO Box 5008 Berkeley CA 94705

"Indigo Animal" has been accepted by the United States Trademark and Patent Office as a
trademark entitled to be registered. Registration is pending.

Excerpts have been previously published in *The Secret Alameda*, Issues #3, 1991;
Issue #5, 1992; Issue #6, 1993; *works+ conversations*, March 1998.

To order by phone call: 510.547.3250
To order by fax: 510.594.8713
To order on line: http://www.PorchLionPress.com
(or use the order form on the last page of this book)

Library of Congress Catalog Card Number: 98-87909
ISBN: 0-9667279-0-8

Printed in USA

Indigo Animal

by
Rue Harrison

PORCH
LION
PRESS
P.O. Box 5008 Berkeley CA 94705

For my Father
&
For Richard

CHAPTER ONE
Indigo Animal

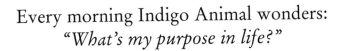

Every morning Indigo Animal wonders:
"What's my purpose in life?"

On long solitary walks Indigo Animal ponders this question and discovers there are no easy answers.

Nevertheless, the beauty of lawn statuary comforts this perhaps overly-serious animal.

Lawn statuary is mysterious.

Maybe it's an expression of the unrealized dreams of its owners.

Indigo Animal doesn't understand why the lawn statuary owners
spend so much time away from the neighborhood.

They drive away each day, full of purpose.

Feeling a little lonely,
Indigo Animal stops to savor
the confident lines
of the Blaylocks' fish fountain.
The Blaylocks themselves left hours ago,
briefcases in hand.

"They must have very important things to do,"
thinks Indigo, walking down
a well-worn path toward home.

CHAPTER TWO
The TV

Once at home Indigo Animal faces a compelling presence.

The TV.

Although Indigo only watches nature programs,

golf,

and the occasional game show,

there never seems to be enough time to get started on something
serious, like an in-depth study of lawn statuary.

CHAPTER THREE
Change

That night as Indigo sleeps,

a vehicle for profound change appears in the form of three squirrels

who have developed an addiction to a late night talk show.

They steal the TV.

The next morning Indigo feels
unperturbed—
even glad—
that the TV's gone.

But by evening Indigo's feelings begin to change.

Several weeks pass, very slowly.

One day, while studying a backyard reliquary,
an amazing thing happens.

The theme tune from "Jeopardy" —
that's been playing in Indigo's head—
stops!

Indigo Animal is energized by heretofore unperceived vibrations.

Pausing at the Head of Zeno fountain,
a new thought comes into focus—*research*.

CHAPTER FOUR

Classical Lawn Statuary Research

Indigo Animal loves classical lawn statuary. It has endured.

The ancients knew the value of a well-appointed garden.

Symmetrical forms are a balm to the spirit.

"Does that mean that they embody truth?"
Indigo Animal wonders.

As the research progresses,

Indigo Animal is able to discern that some statuaries,

although derived from classical forms,

do not produce the optimum enjoyment/satisfaction response.
Why?

Thus, Indigo Animal is led to a study

of ancient systems of proportion.

One night the impassioned creature applies this knowledge
to the most familiar form of all

and discovers that in their own way, the proportions of
the Indigo Animal are attuned to the classical ideal.

On a midnight stroll Indigo Animal looks at the stars and thinks:

"My mind feels like a lawn mower recently delivered
home by a good repairman."

CHAPTER FIVE
Dream Journey

Later that night Indigo Animal dreams about a grand and elaborately-decorated mansion.

Examining the protector statuary at the front gate, Indigo wonders, "How could I have missed this place before?"

The mansion has many handsome details.

Even the topiary has a heroic quality.

Indigo Animal finds the door ajar and steps inside.

There's a hallway filled with stunning works of art.

Some of the paintings are regal and opulent.

Some express purity.

Others celebrate the joys of success.

The hallway ends with a heavy wooden door
surrounded by primitive runes.

Beyond the doors, stairs descend to a dimly-lit cavern.

A single gondola is moored in the murky water.

Indigo Animal decides to take a ride.

The gondola floats along a mild current.

As Indigo's eyes become accustomed to the low light,
the side of the cavern comes alive with images.

As the gondola drifts further, Indigo sees ancient paintings covering the walls of the cave.

For the first time, Indigo feels connected to the Indigo Animals that have gone before. Echoes of their thoughts and feelings seem nearby.

Indigo Animal tries to remain calm as the gondola floats
down an ever-darkening passageway.

In the
inky darkness
the sound of
water droplets
comes alive.
Indigo Animal
listens for
what seems a
very long time.

For one instant, Indigo imagines many hands offering comfort.

And in the next, recognizes them as leaves—part of dense
shrubbery that leads to an open waterway!

Everything Indigo sees in the light of day is cause for celebration!

Then the dream fades into another dream, and
another, on into the morning—

CHAPTER SIX
A Major Discovery

Lawn statuary research
exerts a steady influence
on Indigo Animal's
way of life.

Since new statuaries are appearing in the neighborhood all the time,

Indigo must now get up quite early in order to study
each one and record its specifications.

A certain amount
of brainstorming is also required,
since the style
of many of the pieces
is maddeningly eclectic.

In addition, Indigo Animal
increasingly
feels the impulse to explore streets
that lie beyond
the known territory.

One day, while measuring a birdbath of faintly Etruscan origins,
Indigo spots a colorful object in the grass.

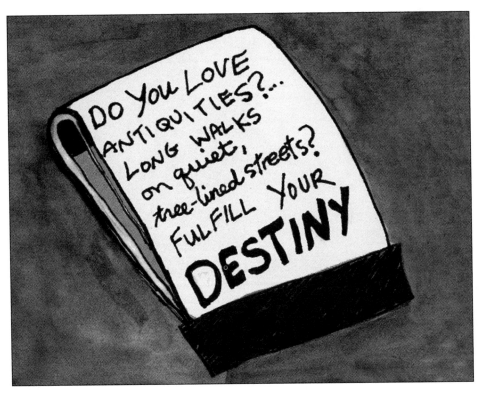

It's a matchbook advertising a special school.

Indigo takes a few deep breaths, feeling the warmth
of the sun and a cool breeze.

Then, in order to assimilate the newly revealed information,
Indigo Animal feels the need to lie down for just a bit.

"Could it really be that somewhere there are others as interested in these statuaries as I am?"

On the way home Indigo Animal arrives at a decision

and with a hopeful heart sends away for the brochure.

CHAPTER SEVEN
Lawn Statuary Research Institute

A few days later the brochure arrives.
Indigo rushes to the shade of a Corinthian portal to read it.

"At Lawn Statuary Research Institute, animals of all stripes

can share their interest in lawn statuary

and explore its subtleties

in an atmosphere of mutual caring and respect.

LSRI's founder, the dynamic theorist and innovator Orange Bearcat,

*has created a curriculum that can lead persevering
animals down rewarding career paths.*

Specializations include:

Country French

Classical

Art Deco

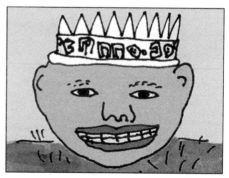
Pre-Colombian

Old English

Japanese

Egyptian

Media Pop

Modern

Post-modern

American Downhome

and Neolithic."

Seeing only one tiny picture
devoted to
Classical Lawn Statuary
in the entire brochure
sets off a mild ontological tremor
in the psyche
of Indigo Animal.
And yet...

how interesting,

how intriguing...

...and ultimately, how thrilling—to imagine that others have become engaged in even a *superficial* attempt to study lawn statuary!

"I'm going to enroll," Indigo Animal resolves. "It's clear from their brochure that they need me to help identify derivative forms."

CHAPTER EIGHT
Which Blanket?

Indigo Animals are creatures of fascinating complexity.
Perhaps that is one way to explain the fact that
Indigo Animal, after so looking forward
to going to LSRI,
wakes up on the first day of class
saturated with a feeling of unspeakable dread,
which quickly transmutes itself
into a series of excuses explaining
why it is no longer necessary
to actually go there.

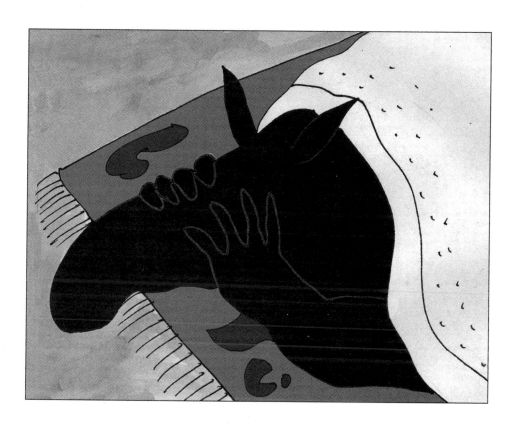

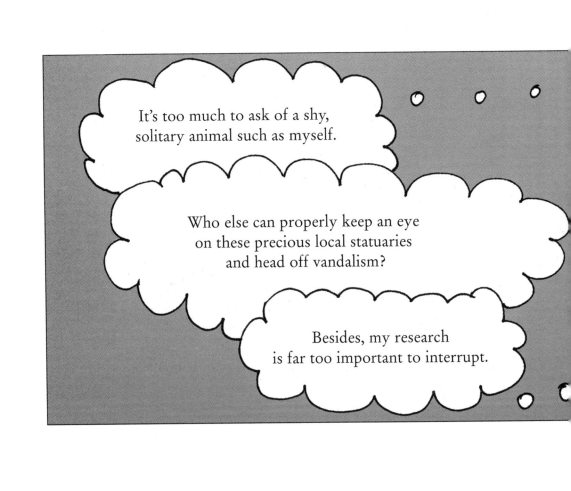

Even as these thoughts flash on and off
in Indigo's brain
like so many lightning bugs,
the long-established morning routine
will not be denied.

And so it happens that during stretching a question begins to free itself from the depths of Indigo Animal's unconscious mind.

It rises closer to the surface during coffee.

And finally breaks through: "If I DID go to LSRI today, which blanket would I wear?"

"Hmm, let's see—in this blanket I can elude notice."

"In this blanket I have gone where no other Indigo Animal
has gone before— and with good reason!"

"This gauzy silk blanket from 'Commes Des Pourceaux'
is too formal for school."

"I've never been able to wear this heli-blanket without crashing."

"What was I thinking when I bought this faux fur blanket?"

"I sent away for this blanket when I got the idea to
climb Everest. But I ended up staying home."

Indigo now notices a very familiar item.

"This is the blanket I was wearing that day the TV was stolen."

"And since I was too depressed to change it for weeks afterwards,"

"it was the one I was wearing when I decided to do research."

"Then I got so involved in research that I just kept on wearing it."

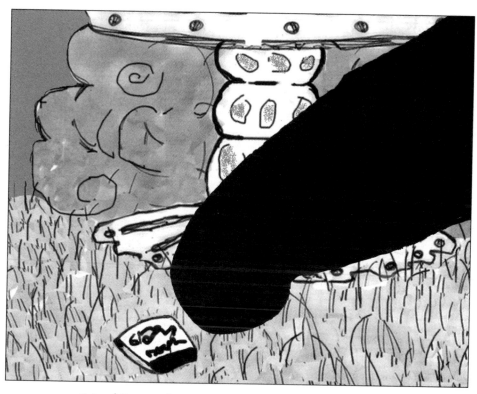

"And I was also wearing it the day I found that matchbook ad for the Institute. And so—"

"This is my POWER BLANKET!!!"

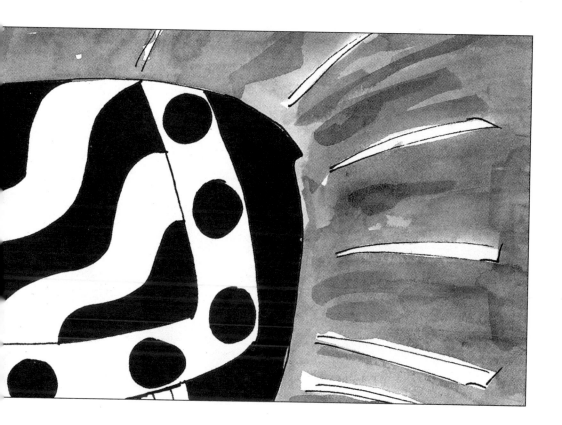

With the familiar pressure of the power blanket
reestablishing earlier hopes and confidence,

Indigo Animal sets off for Lawn Statuary Research Institute—

where the further adventures of INDIGO ANIMAL await!

Visit Indigo Animal online at http://www.IndigoAnimal.com

e-mail for Indigo: Indigo@IndigoAnimal.com

The Author

Porch Lion Press Order Form

Name:_____

Address:_____

City:_____State:_____Zip:_____

I would like to order _____ books at $9.95 per book.
Make checks payable to **Porch Lion Press P.O. Box 5008, Berkeley CA 94705**

Please add 8.25% sales tax for delivery in California.

Shipping:
Book rate: $2.00 for the first book and 75 cents for each additional book
(Surface shipping may take three to four weeks)
Air Mail: $3.50 per book

For further details call 510.547.3250 or e-mail to publisher@PorchLionPress.com
Write c/o Indigo Animal to Porch Lion Press, P.O. Box 5008, Berkeley CA 94705.
Visit Indigo Animal on the web at: http://www.IndigoAnimal.com